# Eighteenth Century Emigrants from Kleingartach in Baden-Württemberg to America

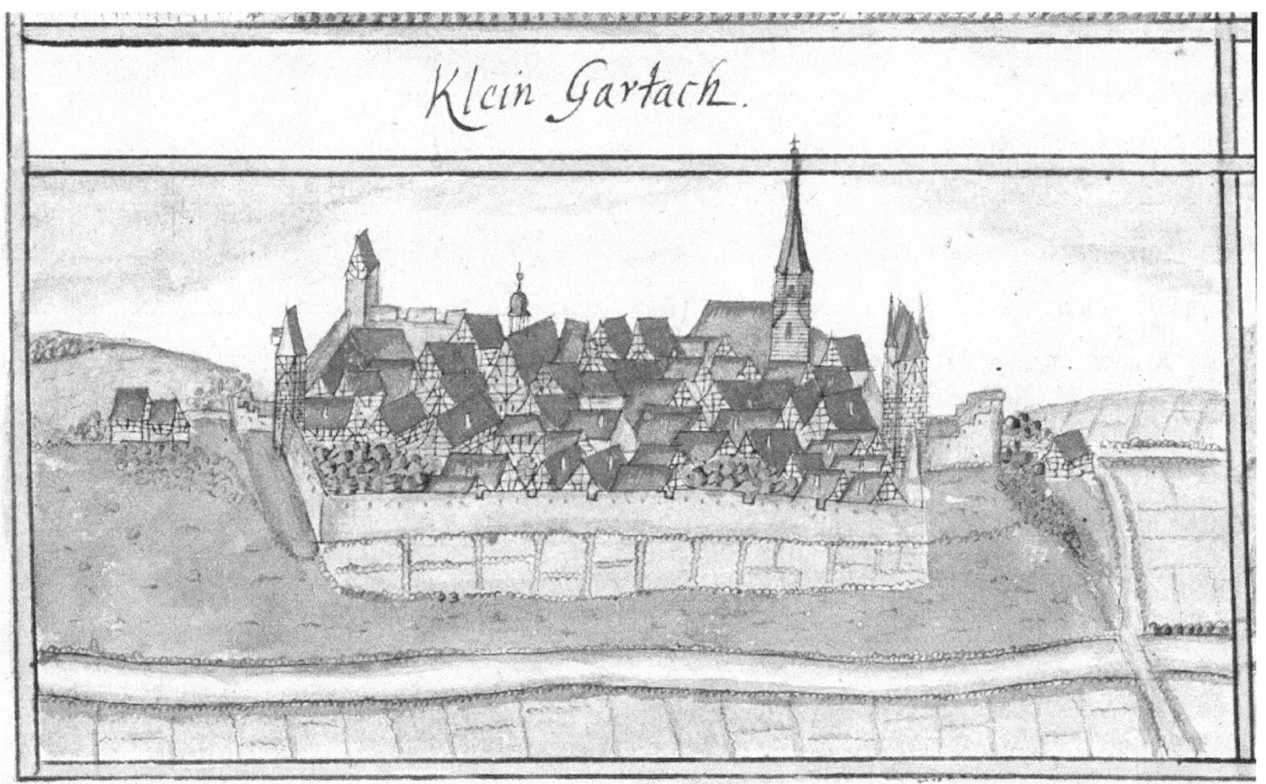


*Kleingartach im Kieserschen Fortslagerbuch, um 1684 (Wikicommons)*

Researched and Compiled by
Edward N. Wevodau

Grapevine, Texas

# Contents

# *Modern Germany identification:*

Ortschaft Kleingartach, Landkreis Heilbronn, Regierungsbezirk Stuttgart, Bundesland Baden-Württemberg, Stat Bundesrepublik Deutschland

(Or)

Kleingartach, Landkreis Heilbronn, Baden-Württemberg, Deutschland

Postal Code: 75031 Kleingartach

*Above: The communities surrounding Heilbronn in Baden-Württemberg. Kleingartach is located within the Stadt Eppingen on the far left. (Source: Wikipedia.de)*

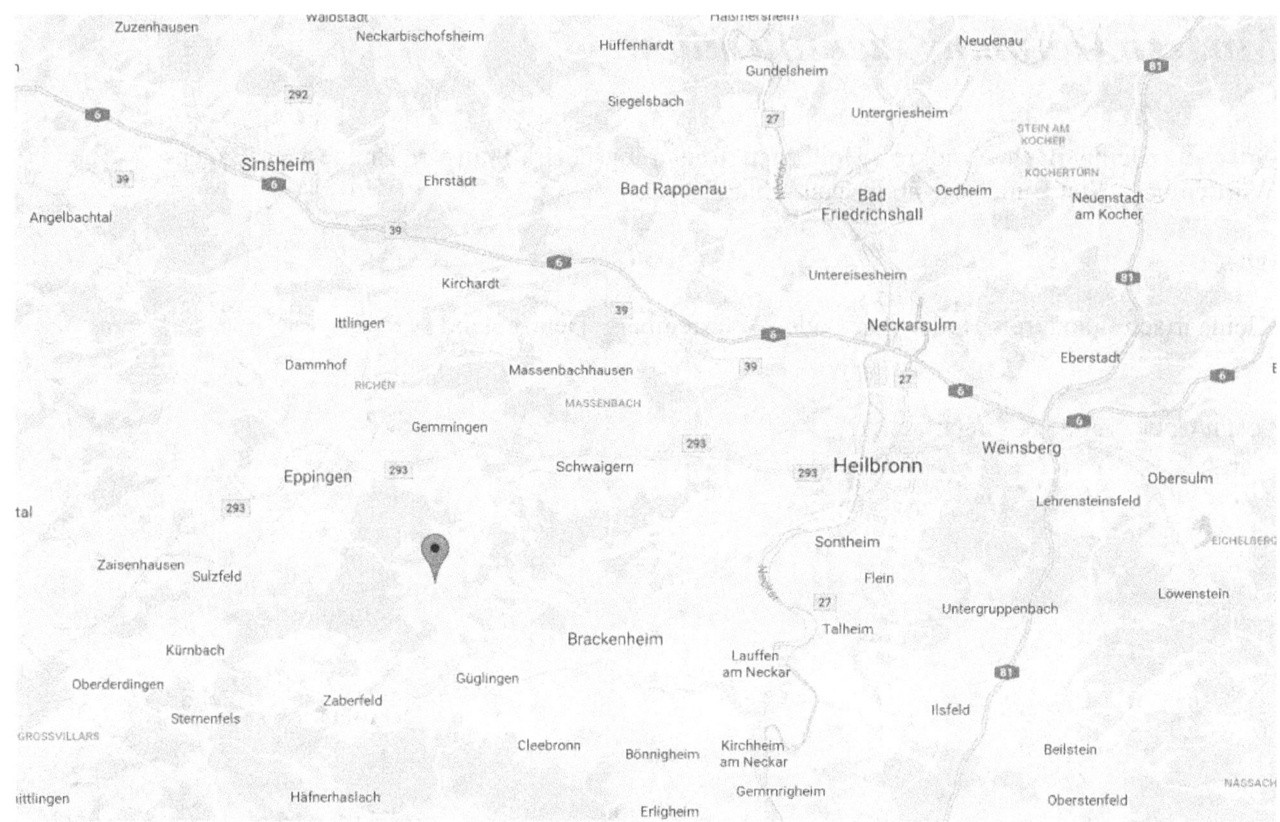

*Above and Below: Google Maps. Kleingartach is located at the red marker.*

In the eighteenth century, several waves of emigrants left the German village of Kleingartach for the American Colonies.  This attempts to document emigrants who settled in the American colonies prior to the onset of the Revolutionary War.

How emigrants were identified:

1. Passenger Lists. All ships arriving at the Port of Philadelphia had to provide a list of all non-British citizens aboard. These immigrants were then administered the Oath of Allegiance to the British Crown, at which time they signed their names to document. Generally, persons who knew each other in Germany (e.g., family, friends, neighbors) stood in line together. When an emigrant from Kleingartach was identified on a passenger list, I searched for all names written above and below in the village church books.
2. American Colonial Records. I searched for evidence of the Kleingartach emigrants in America, compiling all significant findings. When the evidence connected the emigrants to other persons, I investigated the origins of those persons. Germans tended to travel in groups. They departed their homeland together and then settled in America together. In the records compiled below, American baptismal sponsors for the children of emigrants were often from either Kleingartach or neighboring villages.
3. Kleingartach Protestant Church records. I viewed the original Kleingartach Lutheran church records, which are available via digitized microfilm on the website Archion.de.
4. Databases and websites. I used general keyword searches (e.g., "Kleingartach" + Pennsylvania) to locate websites with information related to possible migrations. The websites Ancestry and FamilySearch were used to seek evidence of other researchers who had located eighteenth century emigrants from Kleingartach. I consulted my personal library collection, which has a special emphasis on works related to eighteenth century German emigration.

IMPORTANT: This work should not be considered comprehensive. The church pastors did not typically identify those who left the congregation. Further, no list of emigrants exists in extant German records in the target time period.

 CAVAET: I personally compiled all records cited below from the original Kleingartach Evangelisch church books. This work is among my early efforts at reading old-style German script. I am a beginner— and my translations are subject to error. If these records identify a direct ancestor, I encourage you to access and view the original records on your own to verify the dates and information. I am comfortable navigating basic entries, but when the pastor added unique facts or notes, I often struggled. If I could not read information of possible importance, I copied the original record and indicated my difficulty.


### *The Research of Annette K. Burgert*

Noted immigrant scholar Annette K. Burgert published two works on emigrants from village near to Kleingartach:

> Annette K. Burgert. *Emigrants from Eppingen to American the Eighteenth and Nineteenth Centuries.* AKB Publications. Myerstown, Pennsylvania (1987).

> Annette Kunselman Burgert. *Eighteenth Century Emigrants, Volume I:  The Northern Kraichgau.* The Pennsylvania German Society. Breinigsville, Pennsylvania (1983).

This monograph should be viewed as a complement to Ms. Burgert's research. You have to stop somewhere—her work investigates the church records of German villages adjoining Kleingartach.

KLEINGARTACH PROTESTANT CHURCH RECORDS:


Digitized images of the Kleingartach Evangelisch Church records can be found on the German website
Archion.de. With a paid subscription, the images may be accessed, downloaded, and printed. I consulted
the following digitized books:


***Kleingartach Evangelisch Records (via Archion)***

Mischbuch, 1624-1716:
1. Taufregister (baptisms), 1624-1716
2. Eheregister (marriages), 1649-1716
3. Totenregister (deaths), 1650-1716

Mischbuch, 1716-1765:
1. Taufregister, 1717-1761
2. Eheregister, 1717-1765
3. Totenregister, 1717-1760
4. Seelenregister
5. Angelegt, 1717
6. Kommunikantenregister, 1716-1733

Mischbuch, 1762-1859:
1. Taufregister, 1762-1807
2. Eheregister, 1766-1807
3. Konfirmandenregister, 1763-1859


The LDS Church filmed both of the above church registers. See LDS Films 1184796 and 1184797. *Some*
of the records were abstracted and placed into the LDS's German church records databases.

Ancestry.com has added a searchable database of Württemberg Lutheran church records. Of great value,
each result is linked to a digital image of a page in the original church book.

Ancestry.com. *Württemberg, Germany, Lutheran Baptisms, Marriages, and Burials, 1500-1985*
[database on-line]. Provo, UT, USA: Ancestry.com Operations, Inc., 2016.

| Emigrant | Year | Ship | First Settlement |
|---|---|---|---|
| Bauerschmidt, Jacob | 1752 | Nancy | Lancaster County, Pennsylvania |
| Bauerschmidt, Jacob Jr. | 1752 | Nancy | Lancaster County, Pennsylvania |
| Boeckle, Gottlieb | 1750 | Sandwich | |
| Bucher, Hans Ulrich | 1732 | Plaisance | Opequon in Virginia |
| Bucher, Michael | 1742 | Francis & Elizabeth | Frederick County, Virginia |
| Buehrle, Melchior | 1743 | St. Andrew | Montgomery County, Pennsylvania |
| Jayser, Jacob | 1736 | Harle | Lancaster County, Pennsylvania |
| Jayser, Friederich | 1743 | St. Andrew | Lancaster County, Pennsylvania |
| Jayser, Engelhart | 1750 | Sandwich | Lancaster County, Pennsylvania |
| Jauss, Georg Friederich | 1752 | Nancy | York County, Pennsylvania |
| Krieger, Casper | 1730 | Thistle | Montgomery County, Pennsylvania |
| Kuntzler, Johannes | | | Lancaster County, Pennsylvania |
| Ocker, Ezekial | 1743 | St. Andrew | Philadelphia County, Pennsylvania |
| Plantz, Mattheus | 1742 | Francis & Elizabeth | Lancaster County, Pennsylvania |
| Reichardt, Rudolph | 1732 | Plaisance | Bucks County, Pennsylvania |
| Sorg, Adam | 1752 | President | Lancaster County, Pennsylvania |
| Zugel, George Friederich | 1743 | St. Andrew | Lancaster County, Pennsylvania |
| Zugel, Gottlieb | 1743 | St. Andrew | Lancaster County, Pennsylvania |
| | | | |
| | | | |
| **Possible Emigrants** | | | |
| Seibert, Adam | 1742 | Francis & Elizabeth | |

# Jacob Bauerschmidt

# Jacob Bauerschmidt, Jr.

**1752 Nancy**

Immigrant Jacob Bauerschmidt married four times. He lost his first two wives in Kleingartach. His third wife—Maria Catharina Zügel, daughter of Gottlieb Zügel—may have died during passage or perhaps shortly after arriving at Philadelphia. Jacob Bauerschmidt and his son Jacob signed their names on the passenger list next to Georg Friederich Jaus (q.v.), who was a grandson of the said Gottlieb Zügel.

GERMAN RECORDS:

*Evangelisch, Kleingartach, Neckarkreis, Württemberg:*

Samuel Bauerschmid & his wife Catharina Pommer had baptized:
1.   Hans Jacob, baptized 9 Oct 1708

Jacob Bauerschmid, son of Samuel Bauerschmidt, *burger* here, married ----- 1728 Anna Maria Sorg, daughter of Heinrich Sorg (the prior recorded marriage was dated 16 Nov 1728)

Jacob Bauerschmid & his wife Anna Maria had baptized:
1.   Johann Jacob, born 23 Oct 1729, baptized 23 Oct 1729
2.   Catharina Barbara, born 4 Dec 1731, baptized 5 Dec 1731—died 12 Sep 1734
3.   Elisabetha Barbara, born 7 Apr 1736 (cross next to name)

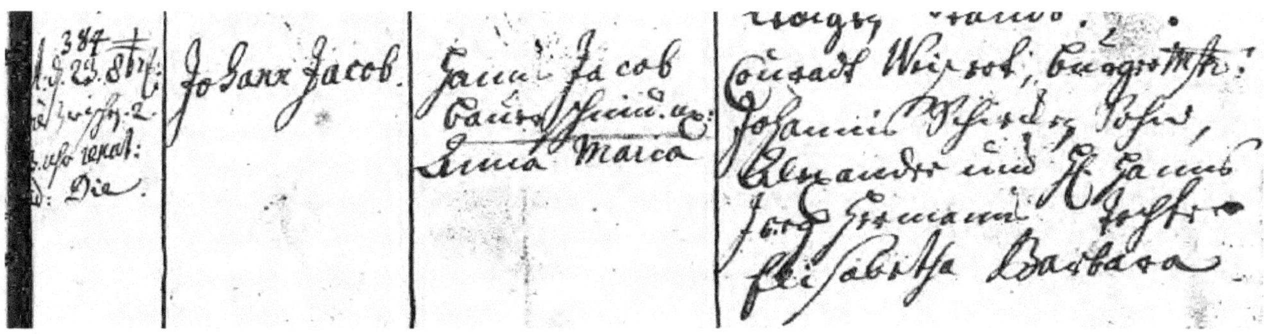

*Above: 1729 Kleingartach baptism of American immigrant Johann Jacob Bauerschmidt. (Source: Ancestry.com)*

Died 9 June 1746: Anna Maria, wife of Hans Jacob Bauerschmid, *weingartner* here, aged 53 years

Married 31 Jan 1747: Jacob Bauerschmid, widower, and Maria Barbara Mertz, daughter of Matthäi Mertz. They had baptized:
1.   Anna Catharina, born 24 Nov 1747—died 11 Nov 1747, aged 14 days [sic]

Died 27 Jan 1748: Maria Barbara, wife of Hans Jacob Bauerschmid, aged 46 years

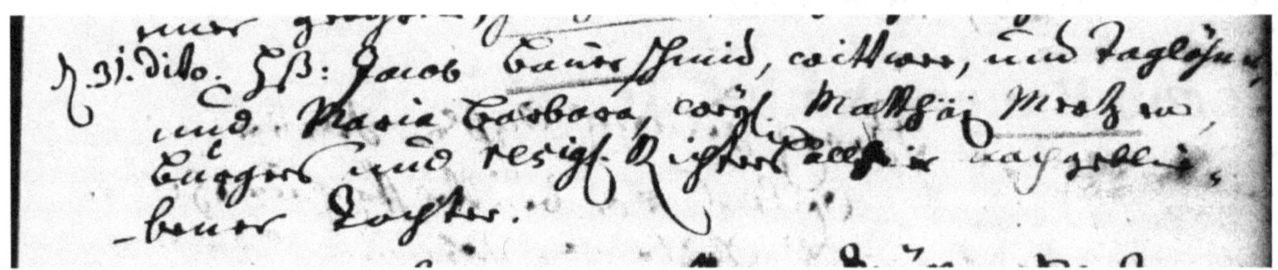

Married 23 July 1748: Jacob Bauerschmid, widower and *burger* here, and Maria Catharina Zügel, daughter of Gottlieb Zuegel. They had baptized:
1. Johann Georg, born -- May 1749 (day of birth in fold on microfilm image)
2. Catharina Barbara, born 12 Jan 1752

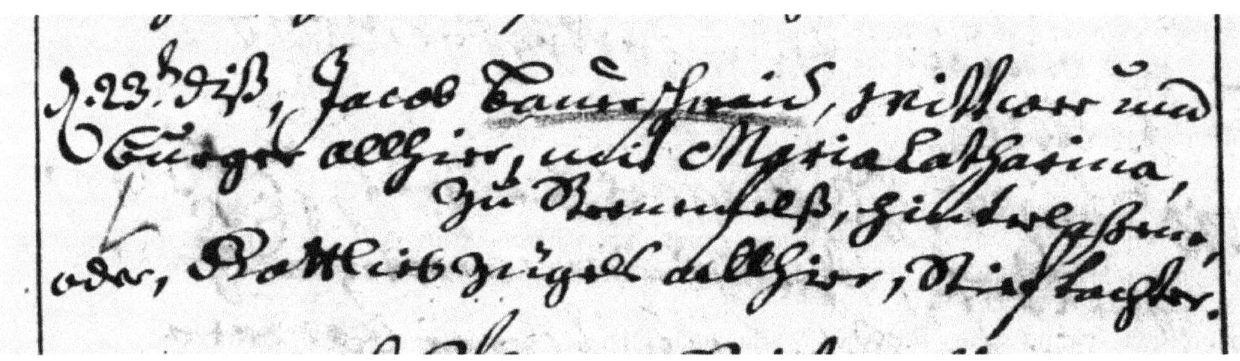

IMMIGRATION:

**Ship *Nancy*, qualified 27 Sep 1752 at Philadelphia:**

Jacob Bauerschmid
Jacob Bauerschmidt
Gerg Friderich Jauss (q.v.)
*--Signed next to each other.*

PENNSYLVANIA, MARYLAND, AND VIRGINIA RECORDS:

***Lancaster (Trinity) Lutheran KB, Lancaster, Lancaster County, Pennsylvania:***

Married 23 July 1753: Jacob Bauerschmidt, widower from Klein Gartach in Württ. and Catharina Ruffin, widow, from Durlach.

*U.S. Federal Census Records:*

1790 Federal Census: *Frederick, Maryland*; Series: *M637*; Roll: *3*; Page: *217*; Image: *493*; Family History Library Film: *0568143*.
Geo. Bowersmith, 1-4-6

1850 Federal Census: Mill Creek, Union County, Ohio
Jacob Bowersmith, age 70 years, born in the State of Virginia

(This Jacob Bowersmith died 18 Apr 1873, buried in Blue Point Baptist Cemetery, Shumway, Effingham County, Illinois, USA. See findagrave.com memorial page. An Ancestry.com family tree identifies this Jacob Bowersmith as the son of a George Bowersmith, 1750-1800, who died in Maryland.)


*Loudoun County, Virginia, Marriages:*

Jacob Bowersmith married 20 July 1815 Matilda Jenkins

# Gottlieb Böckle (or Boeckle)

**1750 Sandwich**

Engelhard Jaÿser (or Jaiser) [q.v.] arrived at Philadelphia in 1750 aboard the Ship *Sandwich*. His wife Eva was the daughter of Raymund Böckle of nearby Güglingen. Appearing next to Engelhard on the passenger list was a Gottlieb Beckly (who could not sign his name). Eva's father Raymund did have a son named Gottlieb born in 1731. It would be reasonable to conclude that passenger on the Sandwich was Raymund's son; however, a Gottlieb Böckle, son of Raymund, married at Güglingen in 1753.

Occasionally, Pennsylvania Germans returned to their homeland. Then again, perhaps the Sandwich passenger was born to a different Böckle family from the same region in Germany.

Further research is necessary to determine the origin of this Gottlieb Böckle.

GERMAN RECORDS:

***Evangelisch, Guglingen, Neckarkreis, Württemberg:***

Married 8 Sep 1711: Johann Raimundus Böckle, Metzger, son of Johann Raimundus Böckle, resident here, and Maria Magdalena, daughter of Andrea Buckert, resident here.

Johann Raymund Boecklen & his wife Maria Magdalena had baptized:
1. Eva, born 2 June 1719, baptized 3 June 1719
2. Gottlieb, born 10 Sep 1731, baptized 11 Sep 1731

*--Note: Other children not compiled.*

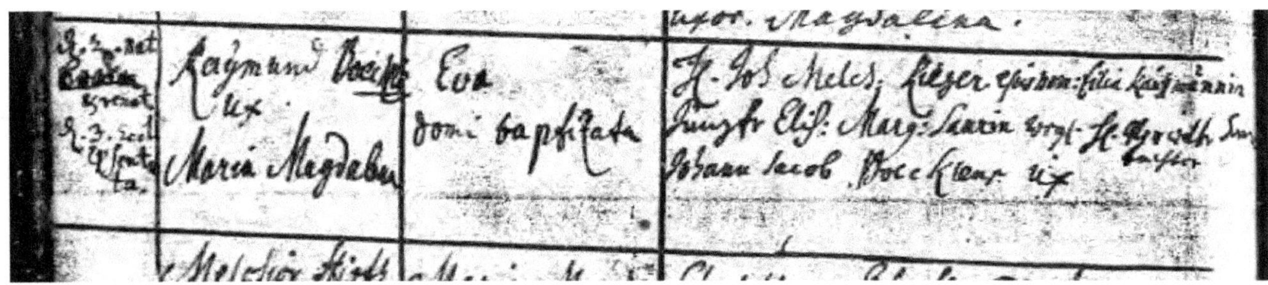

*Above: 1719 Guglingen baptism of Eva Boeckle. (Source: Ancestry.com)*

Married 6 Oct 1739: Engelhard Jaiser, son of Johann Jacob Jaiser, married 6 Oct 1739 Eva Boecklen, daughter of Raymund Boecklen

Married 19 June 1753: Gottlieb Böckle, son of Raymund Böcklen, and Eva Magdalena, daughter of David Ezel

IMMIGRATION:

**Ship *Sandwich*, qualified 30 Nov 1750 at Philadelphia:**

Engelhart (X) Yeiser
Godlieb (X) Beckly
--Signed next to each other.

*Note: If the Godlieb Beckly above was Gottlieb Boecklen, son of Raymund Boecklen and brother of Eva Jaisser, then he must have returned to Güglingen by June 1753, where he married Eva Magdalena Ezel. I did not locate another Gottlieb Böckle in the Güglingen church records.*

*A Gottlieb Boeckle & wife Margretha had a son Johannes, born 13 Apr 1768, baptized at St. Michael's and Zion Lutheran Church in Philadelphia.*

COLONIAL RECORDS:

Not located.

# Hans Ulrich Bucher

# Johann Michael Bucher

**1732 Pink Plaisance (Ulrich Bucher)**
**1742 Francis and Elizabeth (Michael Bucher)**

Charles Lee Booker  has published a thorough and well-documented book on the Bucher family:

> Charles Lee Booker. *The Bucher/Booker family, 1686-1990 : from Klein Gartach, Wurttemberg, Germany to Frederick county, Virginia to Harrison and Jefferson counties, Kentucky to Knox and Sullivan counties, Indiana to the Illinois counties of Jasper, Macon, Moultrie, Piatt, and Sangamon.* Published by C.L. Booker, c1990. 828 pages. [See LDS online catalogue. Available via LDS film 1697778.]

Mr. Booker includes a transcription of a document dated 2 May 1742 at Kleingartach.

*"... Michael Bucher, yet unmarried, legitimate son of Ulrich Bucher, former citizen and tailor of this place who left here in 1732 and emigrated to Pennsylvania. This deponent stated he desired also to go to Pennsylvania and help seek his father, decided with God's divine help. To this end, he humbly requests a certificate verifying his legitimate birth in this place and his good conduct during his residence here so that he may show this document during his travels for purposes of safe conduct....."*

GERMAN RECORDS

*Evangelisch, Kleingartach, Neckarkreis, Baden-Württemberg:*

Hans Ulrich Bucher von Michelbach married 7 Mar 1713 Anna Maria Schellinger of this place. They had baptized:
1. Johann Michael, born 17 Aug 1715, baptized 18 Aug 1715
2. Georg Heinrich, born 18 June 1718, baptized 19 June 1718

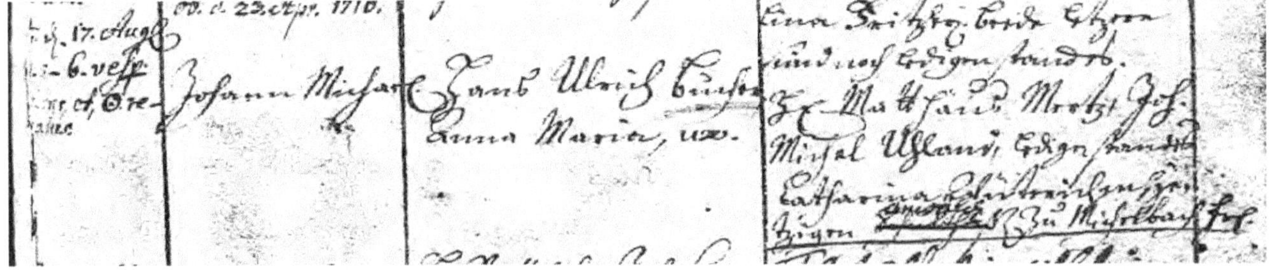

*Above: 1715 Kleingartach baptism of Johann Michael Bucher (Source: Ancestry.com)*

Married 17 Apr 1725: Ulrich Bucher, widower,. and Anna Barbara, daughter of Johann Wirth, burger zu Craylshause (?) [see image]

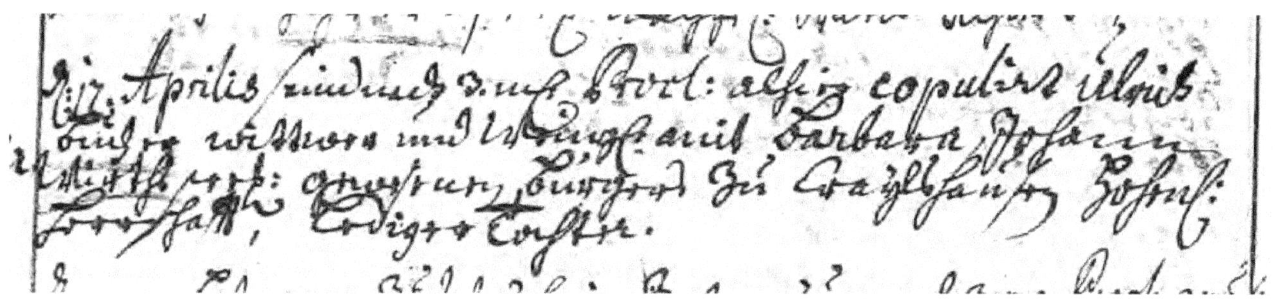

*Source: Ancestry.com*

Ulrich Bucher & his wife Anna Barbara had baptized:
1. Margaretha Barbara, born 20 Jan 1726, baptized 20 Jan 1726
2. Johann Philipp, born 12 May 1728, baptized 12 May 1728
3. Catharina, born 26 June 1730, baptized 27 June 1730

IMMIGRATION:

***Pink Plaisance, qualified 21 Sep 1732 at Philadelphia:***

Hans Ulrich Bucher, age 45 (signed his name)
Barbara Bogarey, age 35
Margaret Bugarin (aged not given)

**Ship *Francis and Elisabeth*, qualified 21 Sep 1742 at Philadelphia:**

Melcher Schöner
Hans Michael Doll
John Michael Bucher
Abraham Groff
Johann Michael Seitz

VIRGINIA RECORDS:

***Stoever, Rev. John Casper, personal register:***

Johann Ulrich Buger of the Opequon settlement had baptized:
1. Rosina, born 9 Feb 1735, baptized 16 May 1735, sp. Jost Heydt, Susanna Weismanenn, and Barbara Schnäppin
2. Johannes, born --- Nov 1736, baptized 5 June 1737, sp. Jost Heydt & his wife Anna Maria and John Schnepp
3. Jacob, born 29 Apr 1739, baptized 29 Apr 1739, sp. Jost Heydt and Barbara Schneppin

Carl Ehrhardt and Susanna Barbara Buger sponsored child of Rudi Magg on 2 May 1736
Philipp Schless and Barbara Buger sponsored child of Johannes Schnepf on 15 June 1739
Ulrich Buger and Barbara Schnepf sponsored child of Lorentz Schnepf on 29 Apr 1740


***Frederick County, Virginia, Estate Records:***

Frederick Will 1-436:
John Wolderick Poker, yeoman, of Frederick County, writ 1 July 1747.
1. "being in a state of good health"
2. To my eldest son Michael Poker: The sum of five shillings. ("for he has had his portion before leaving his mother in Germany")
3. To my next eldest son Philip Poker and my youngest son George Poker: All my I have in the Colony of Virginia together with the buildings thereon.
4. The aforesaid land shall be valued and appraised by my executors. My said sons shall then pay equal shares of this valuation unto each of their brothers and sisters, viz.: Alexander, John, Jacob, Barbara, and Rosana Poker.
5. To my loving wife Barbara: All my estate both real and personal during her natural life or so long as she remains my widow.
6. Executors: John Snap, Sr., George Dellinger, and John Hite.
7. Signed his name with a mark.


**From the book, *The Lutheran Church in Virginia 1717-1962*, by William Edward Eisenberg, published in 1967, page 25:**

"[Rev.] *Klug labored on both east and west sides of the Massanutten and went beyond Strasburg into the Opequon - Cedar Creek Settlement. When on November 5, 1746, John Snapp, John Snapp, Sr., Lawrence Snapp and John Ulrich Bucher, were naturalized by the Frederick County Court, they all testified that they had received the Lord's Supper from Pastor Klug and produced certificates with his signature thereon. The next spring at a May 5th court, John George Dellinger, Phillip Glass (Kleez), Jacob Peck, Augustine Windle [married Ulrich Bucher's daughter, Anna Margaretha], Christopher Windle, Peter Mauk [and others]...Phillip Boucher [sic] and Michael Boucher [sic] all presented similar testimony in order to obtain naturalization. All these had been in the Opequon settlement seven years or more, the children of many of them having been baptized by J. C. Stoever, Jr.*"

# Melchior Bührle

**1743 St. Andrew**

Melchior Buhrle arrived at Philadelphia in 1743, signing his name to the passenger list of the St. Andrew next to his brother-in-law Ezekial Ocker (q.v.). Melchior and his wife were the next of kin and sole heirs of Ezekial's estate. His children adopted the spelling *Bierly*.

GERMAN RECORDS:

***Kleingartach Evangelisch KB:***

Hans Martin Ockher (or Oker) & his wife Anna Barbara Schmid had baptized:
1.  Magdalena Regina, born 28 Feb 1703, baptized 2 Mar 1703
2.  Ezechiel, born 11 June 1706, baptized 12 June 1706
3.  Maria Catharina, born 2 Jan 1709, baptized 3 Jan 1709
4.  Maria Barbara, born April 1711, baptized April 1711

Married 15 July 1738: Johann Melchior Bihrlen (?), son of [omitted] Bihren, burger at Bettlingen…..and Maria Barbara Ocker, daughter of Martin Ocker, *bauermann*, here

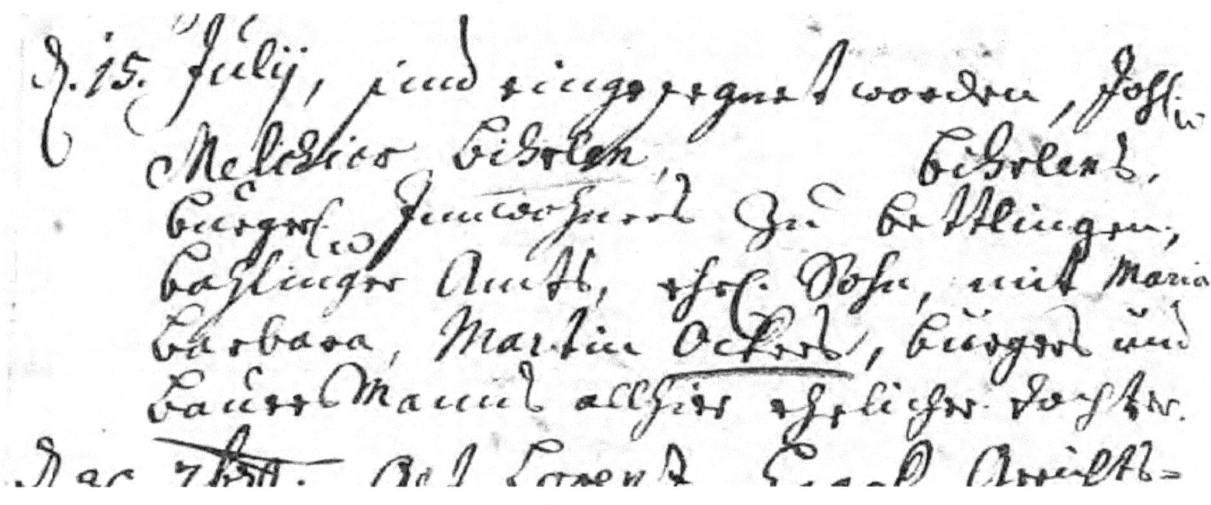



Melchior Bührle  & his wife Maria Barbara had baptized:
1.  Catharina Barbara, born --- Aug 1739, baptized – Aug 1739 (day lost in fold on microfilm image)
2.  Johanna Friderica, born 10 Mar 1742, baptized 10 Mar 1742

IMMIGRATION:

**Ship _St. Andrew_, qualified 7 Oct 1743 at Philadelphia:**

Hans Gerg (X) Amon, age 38
Melchior Bührle, age 30
Etielle Acker, age 39 (given as Ezekial on List A)
Johannes (HU) Ulrich, age 38
Frederick (X) Hubely, age 25


PENNSYLVANIA RECORDS:

_**New Hanover Lutheran KB, Montgomery County, Pennsylvania:**_

Melchior Bierle & his wife Barbara had baptized:
1.  Valentina Elisabeth, born 24 Oct 1744, baptized 18 Nov 1744, sp. Valentine Rupert & his wife
2.  Maria Barbara, born 26 Jan 1746, baptized 30 Mar 1746, sp. Yelden Ruppert & his wife Elisabeth
3.  Joh. Antoni, born 22 Dec 1747, baptized 5 June 1748, sp. Antoni Geiger & Barbara Geiger


_**Northumberland County, Pennsylvania, Tax lists:**_

Melchior Bierly, 1772, Augusta Township
Anthony Bierly, 1772, Augusta Township
Nicholas Bierly, 1772, Augusta Township

# Jacob Jayser (or Jaisser)

# Friederich Jayser (or Jaisser)

# Engelhart Jayser (or Jaisser)

Hans Jacob Jaÿser (or Jaysser, Jaisser, Jaiser) and his wife Anna Barbara of Kleingartach saw at least four children emigrate to the American colonies, where they lived in or near the Borough of Lancaster in Lancaster County, Pennsylvania. Those children are as follows:
1. Son Jacob, arrived at Philadelphia on board the Ship *Harle* in 1736.
2. Son Christian Friederich, arrived at Philadelphia on board the Ship *St. Andrew* in 1743.
3. Son Engelhart, arrived at Philadelphia on board the Ship *Sandwich* in 1750.
4. Daughter Justina Magdalena, in Lancaster by 1748, likely arrived with her brother Christian Friederich in 1743.

Justina Magdalena Jaÿser married the widower Philipp Schütz in Pennsylvania. Neither had children who survived to adulthood. Their last will and testaments (see below) help tie the relationships of the different Jaÿser immigrants together in Pennsylvania.

This family was prominent in Lancaster in the mid-eighteenth century and actively involved with Trinity Lutheran Church.


GERMAN RECORDS:

***Evangelisch, Kleingartach, Neckarkreis, Württemberg:***

Johannes Sachenheimer & his wife Anna Maria had baptized:
1. Anna Barbara, born 4 Sep 1689, baptized 5 Sep 1689

Hans Jacob, son of Hans Jacob Jaÿser, married 16 Feb 1706 Anna Barbara, daughter of Johann Saxenheimer. (See image below for residences.)

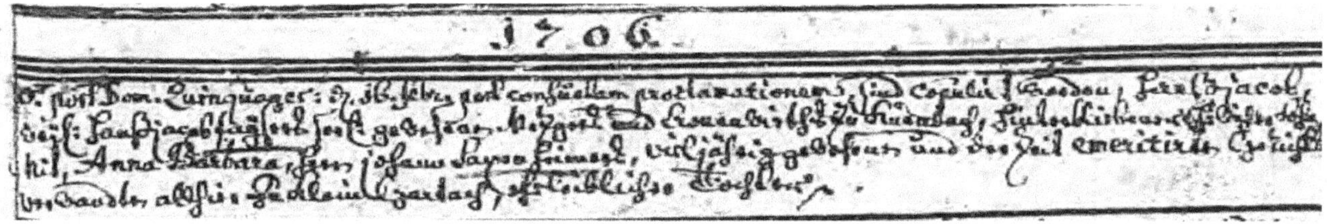

Hans Jacob Jaÿser (or Jaiser) & his wife Anna Barbara had baptized:
1. Anna Barbara, born June 1708, baptized June 1708

2.  Johann Engelhart, born 11 Oct 1709, baptized 12 Oct 1709
3.  Hans Jacob, born 16 Dec 1712, baptized 17 Dec 1712
4.  Johanna, born 27 Dec 1714, baptized 28 Dec 1714
5.  Conrad, born 18 Feb 1716, baptized 19 Feb 1716
6.  Justina Magdalena, born 25 Feb 1717, baptized 26 Feb 1717
7.  Juliana, born 22 Mar 1719, baptized 24 Mar 1719
8.  Eva Elisabetha, born 15 July 1720, baptized 16 July 1720
9.  Rosina, born 4 Feb 1722, baptized 6 Feb 1722
10. Christian Friderich, born 20 Oct 1723, baptized 22 Oct 1723

*Below: The Kleingartach baptismal entries for American immigrants Engelhart Jayser, Jacob Jayser, Justina Magdalena Jayser, and Christian Friderich Jayser:*

*1709*

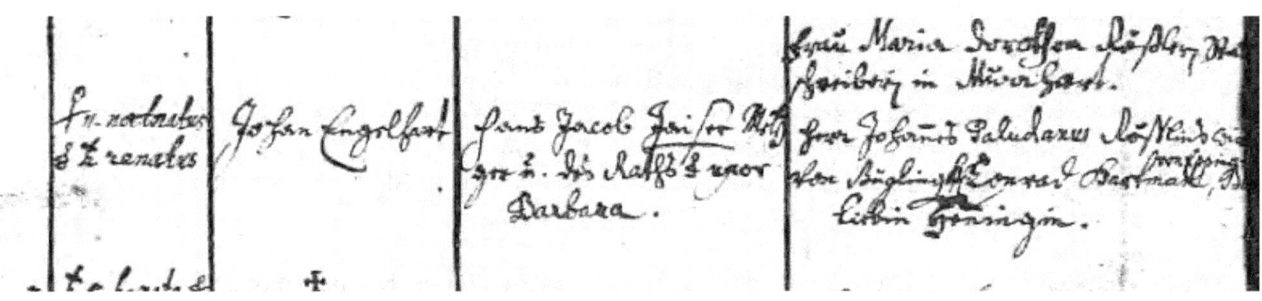

*1712*

*1717*

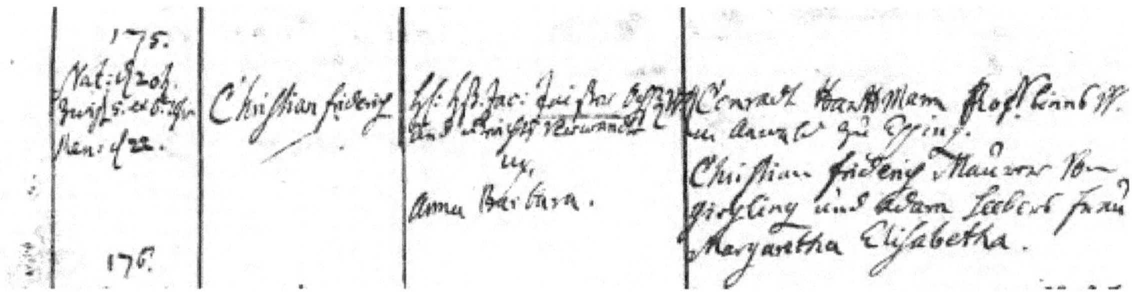

Engelhardt Jaiser & his wife Eva had baptized:
1.  Jacob, born – Sep 1740
2.  Engehardt, born 17 Apr 1742—died 14 Jan 1745
3.  Johannes, born 27 June 1746

***Evangelisch, Pfaffenhofen, Württemberg:***

Married 12 Feb 1743: Matthaus Köller, son of Friderich Köller, burger and bauer here, and Eva, daughter of Johann Jacob Jaisser of Kl. Gartach

***Evangelisch, Guglingen, Neckarkreis, Württemberg:***

Johann Raymund Boecklen & his wife Maria Magdalena had baptized:
1.  Gottlieb, born 10 Sep 1731, baptized 11 Sep 1731

Engelhard Jaiser, son of Johann Jacob Jaiser, married 6 Oct 1739 Eva Boecklen, daughter of Raymund Boecklen

IMMIGRATION:

**Ship *Harle*, qualified 1 Sep 1736:**

Jacob Jayser, age 23 (signed his name)

**Ship *St. Andrew*, qualified 7 Oct 1743 at Philadelphia:**

Friederich Jayser, age 20 (signed his name)

**Ship *Sandwich*, qualified 30 Nov 1750 at Philadelphia:**

Engelhart (X) Yeiser
Godlieb (X) Beckly
--Signed next to each other.

*Note: If the Godlieb Beckly above was Gottlieb Boecklen, son of Raymund Boecklen and brother of Eva Jaisser, then he must have returned to Güglingen by June 1753, where he married Eva Magdalena Ezel.*

*A Gottlieb Boeckle & wife Margretha had a son Johannes, born 13 Apr 1768, baptized at St. Michael's and Zion Lutheran Church in Philadelphia.*


PENNSYLVANIA RECORDS:


***New Holland Lutheran KB, Earl Township, Lancaster County, Pennsylvania:***

Jacob Jaÿsser & his wife Margaretha Barbara sponsored child of Michael Probst on 13 Sep 1745


***Lancaster (Trinity) Lutheran KB, Lancaster, Lancaster County, Pennsylvania:***

Friedrich Jaiser & his wife Catharina had baptized:
1. Magdalena, born 5 Jan 1751, baptized 7 Jan 1751, sp. Philipp Schütz & his wife Magdalena
2. Johann Friederich, born 4 July 1756, baptized 11 July 1756, sp. Johannes Schwaab & his wife Catharina
3. Catharina, born 22 Jan 1761, baptized 25 Jan 1761, sp. Gerhart Brenner and Magdalena Schüzin


Magdalena, little daughter of Friedrich Jayser & Catharina, born 5 Jan, baptized 7 Jan, died 14 Jan. Buried 16 Jan 1751.

Christian Friederich Jayser, an elder, aged 38 years, 5 months, 22 days, died 11 Apr 1762. Buried on Easter Monday.

Catharina, surviving daughter of the late Friederich Jayser, affected with convulsions and a lame arm, died 27 Sep 1766, buried Sunday afternoon, aged 5 years, 8 months, and 5 days.

Friederich Jayser & Magdalena Schützin sponsored child of Heinrich Süss & his wife Charlotta on 3 Feb 1754 and 30 Nov 1755

Friederich Jeyser, Elisabeth Grossin, and Eva Hubelin sponsored child of Joh. Siegfried Gerock, Pastor, & his wife Rosina on 7 Oct 1756


Elected deacon, 4 Aug 1751: Friederich Jaÿsser (signed his name)

---------------------------------------------------------

Engelhart Jayser & his wife Eva had baptized:

1.  Eva Rosina, born 18 Aug 1754, baptized 24 Aug 1754, sp. Wilhelm Göbel & his wife Eva Elisabeth


Eva Rosina, daughter of Engelhart Jayser, aged 9 years, 2 months, died 18 Oct 1763 and buried the following day.

Riemer Land, practitioner of physic, of Lancaster Borough married 22 July 1764 Eve Yaisser, widow

Engelhardt Jaiser & his wife sponsored child of Philip Heilbauer & his wife Anna Barbara on 6 June 1751

Engelhard Jaiser & his wife Eva sponsored child of Joseph Klepfer & his wife Anna Christina on 18 Feb 1753 and 28 Apr 1754

Engelhart Jayser & his wife Eva sponsored child of Joh. George Marquart & his wife Maria Catharina on 14 Oct 1753 and 7 Mar 1756

Engelhart Jeisser & his wife sponsored child of Johannes Würmle & his wife Maria on 13 Jan 1754 and [1755] and 8 May 1757

Eva Jeyserin, Bernhart Hubele, and Elisabet Grossin sponsored child of Joh. Siegfried Gerock, Pastor, & his wife Rosina on 16 Mar 1755

Engelhart Jayser & his wife Eva sponsored child of Jacob Eichholz & his wife Catharina on 25 Jan 1756 and 16 Oct 1757

Engelhart Jayser & his wife Eva sponsored child of Christoph Gruys & his wife Catharina on 26 Mar 1758

Engelhart Jayser & his wife Eva sponsored child of Christian Würtz & his wife Margaret on 28 July 1758 and 27 Jan 1760

Engelhart Jayser & his wife Eva sponsored child of Peter Kieffer & his wife Catharina on 30 July 1758

Eva Jayserin, widow, sponsored child of Heinrich Gross & his wife Anna Maria on 14 Feb 1762

-------------------------------------------------------------

Jacob F. Yaisser, butcher, married 27 Apr 1762 Rebecca Kunz, spinster

Jacob Jayser & his wife Margaret had baptized:
1.  [Name not given], born [no date], baptized 3 Feb 1765, sp. [none listed]

Jacob Jayser, a young married man, died of tuberculosis, 21 Apr 1766, buried the following day.

-------------------------------------------------

*Lancaster Moravian KB (contained within first volume of Lutheran church book)*

Jacob Jaÿser & his wife Margaret sponsored  child of Philip Adam Dambach & his wife Regina on 18 Dec 1743

Jacob Jayser, Jacob Spanseiler, and Catharina Beyerlin sponsored child of Joseph David Trissler & his wife on 2 Sep 1744

Jacob Jayser & his wife sponsored child of Jacob Müller on 16 Sep 1744


Communicant List Entries in Volume 1 (glanced over): 386 387 365 370


***Lancaster County, Pennsylvania, Orphans Court records:***

Estate of Englehart Yeisser (also Yaisser), late of Lancaster Borough:
1.  Proceedings dated 7 Dec 1762: Petition of Administrator Eve Yaisser (the widow): Said Englehart Yaisser died intestate seized in possession of a house & lot on King St. in Lancaster Borough. The petitioner requests to sell this property in order to pay debts. Ordered by the Court to sell on 24 Dec instant.
2.  Proceedings dated first Tuesday March 1763: Report from Administrator Eve Yeisser: On 17 Dec last she sold a house & lot on King St. in Lancaster Borough to Jacob Yeisser (the highest bidder).

Estate of Frederick Yaisser (also Yeisser, Yaiser, Yeiser, Yeizer), late of Lancaster Borough:
1.  Proceedings dated 8 Oct 1762:  Petition of Administrator Catharine Yaisser: Said Frederick Yaisser died intestate seized in possession of a messuage and lot on King St. in Lancaster Borough, then in the tenure of John Stone. The petitioner requests permission to make necessary repairs to the property, especially pertaining to the roof, for the benefit of the estate.
2.  Proceedings dated first Tuesday March 1763: Application of Administrator Catharine Yeisser: She has leased a messuage & half lot on King St. in Lancaster Borough to John Stone for the term of six years (upcoming from 1 Oct last).
3.  Proceedings dated 9 Aug 1766:  Minor Child: Englehart Yeizer (above 14) chooses Michael Hubley, Esq. as guardian.
4.  Proceedings dated 4 June 1767:  Administrator Adam Reigart produces an account. The court approves the balance. Distribution ordered to the Catharine (the late widow) now wife of the said Adam Reigart, Engelhart Yaiser (the eldest son), Philip Yaiser, & Frederick Yaiser. Another daughter, Catharine Yaiser, has since died in her minority, unmarried and without issue.
5.  (A lengthy series of additional entries pertaining to this estate are recorded on the record through the year 1777.)


***Lancaster County, Pennsylvania, Probate Records:***

Lancaster Will A130:
Jacob Yisar of the Borough of Lancaster, writ 23 Mar 1746/47, probated 3 June 1747.
1.  "being sick and weak in body"
2.  To his wife Barbara: All my personal estate as well as houses, lots, and lands in Lancaster or elsewhere to hold to her heirs & assigns forever.
3.  Executor: Wife Barbara.
4.  Signed his name as Jacob Yisar.
5.  Witnessed by David Stout, Michael Fortinee, and Paul Witsel.

Lancaster Will B360:
Philip Schutz, saddler, of the Borough of Lancaster, writ 11 July 1761, probated 2 Sep 1761.
1. "being aged and weak in body"
2. To his wife Magdalena: The western moiety or half part of my lot or piece of ground situate on King Street in Lancaster Borough whereon I now live, together with the buildings thereon.
3. To his wife Magdalena: The eastern moiety or half part of the aforesaid lot during the term of her natural life. After her decease, the property shall go unto Englehart Yeisar, Philip Yeisar, and Frederick Yeisar—the children of Frederick Yeisar of Lancaster Borough. (The children are unmarried minors—if any should die, his share is to be divided amongst the survivors. If all should die, then the property shall go to any surviving child of the father Frederick Yeisar.)
4. To his brother Fredk. Schutz of Bishser (?) in the Electorate Palatine in High Germany: The sum of 150 pounds lawful money of Pennsylvania.
5. To his sister Catharine, wife of Nicholas Fredek, of Bisherer, aforesaid: The sum of 150 pounds lawful money of Pennsylvania.
6. To his sister Eva Maria, wife of Christopher Sheer, of Bisherer, aforesaid: The sum of 150 pounds lawful money of Pennsylvania.
7. Executors: Wife Magdalena and trusty friends Emanuel Carpenter and William Bowsman.
8. Signed his name as Philip Schutz.
9. Codicil dated 30 Aug 1761: He removes William Bowsman as one of the executors.
10. Note: In her work Eighteenth Century Emigrants from the Northern Kraichgau, Annette K. Burgert identified Philip Schutz's German village of birth as Neckarbischofsheim. The siblings named above appear in the church books of that village.

Lancaster Will  F172:
Magdalena Shitz, widow, of the Borough of Lancaster, writ 16 Apr 1787, probated 10 Nov 1789.
1. "being old and weak of body"
2. To Mary Yeizer, one of the daughters of my nephew Frederick Yeizer: The sum of 25 pounds money in gold or silver coin.
3. To my nephew John Yeizer, son of my deceased brother Englehard Yeizer: The sum of 25 pounds money in gold or silver coin.
4. To my nephew Jacob Foltz: The sum of 25 pounds money in gold or silver coin.
5. To my nephews Englehard Yeizer and Philip Yeizer (sons of my deceased brother Frederick Yeizer): All that my house and half lot of ground situate in the Borough of Lancaster on King Street. They also receive the residue of her personal estate.
6. All the rest of my relations are excluded and debarred from having or claiming any share or shares.
7. Executor: Nephew Englehard Yeizer.
8. Signed his name as Magdalena Shitz.
9. Witnessed by Jacob Shindle and Casper Shaffner.


***Lancaster County, Pennsylvania, Deed Records:***

Lancaster Deed MM-263: Englehart Yeiser, innkeeper, of Lancaster Borough
        --Lot on King St. in Lancaster Borough: HISTORY: Same lot that James Hamilton devised one moiety to his wife Magdalena and the other moiety to Englehart Yeiser devised her moiety to the said Englehart Yeiser & Philip Yeiser. On 26 June 1790, Philip Yeiser & his wife Catharine granted their right & title to Englehart Yeiser, giving him full right to the property. [Note: No explanation given as to what happened to the right & title of Frederick Yeiser.]
        --26 June 1790

# Georg Friederich Jauss

**1752 Nancy**

Georg Friederich Jauss's maternal grandfather Gottlieb Zügel had two sons—Gottlieb and Georg Friederich—who also settled in York County, Pennsylvania. Further, Gottlieb Zügel's daughter Maria Catharina married Jacob Bauerschmid, with whom Georg Friederich Jauss traveled to the New World. The German surname *Jauss* (or *Jaus*) is sometimes Anglicized to *Youse*.

GERMAN RECORDS:

***Hattenhofen Evangelisch KB:***

Hans Jorg Jauss & his wife Anna Maria had baptized:
1. Hans Jorg, born 28 Aug 1707, baptized 28 Aug 1707

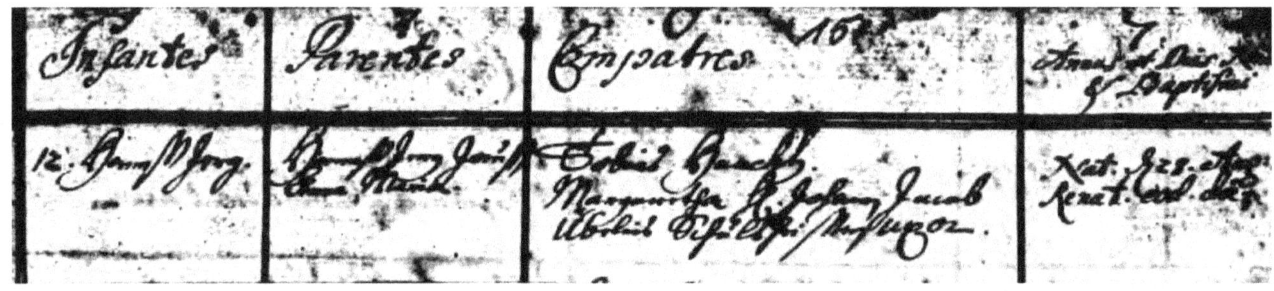

*Source: Ancestry.com*

***Kleingartach Evangelisch KB:***

Married 29 Jan 1732: Johann Georg Jaus, *schmid*, son of Hans Jerg Jaus, *burger und bauermann* at Hattenhofen [?--see image] and Eva Catharina Zuegel, daughter of Gottlieb Zügel, *burger und schmid* here

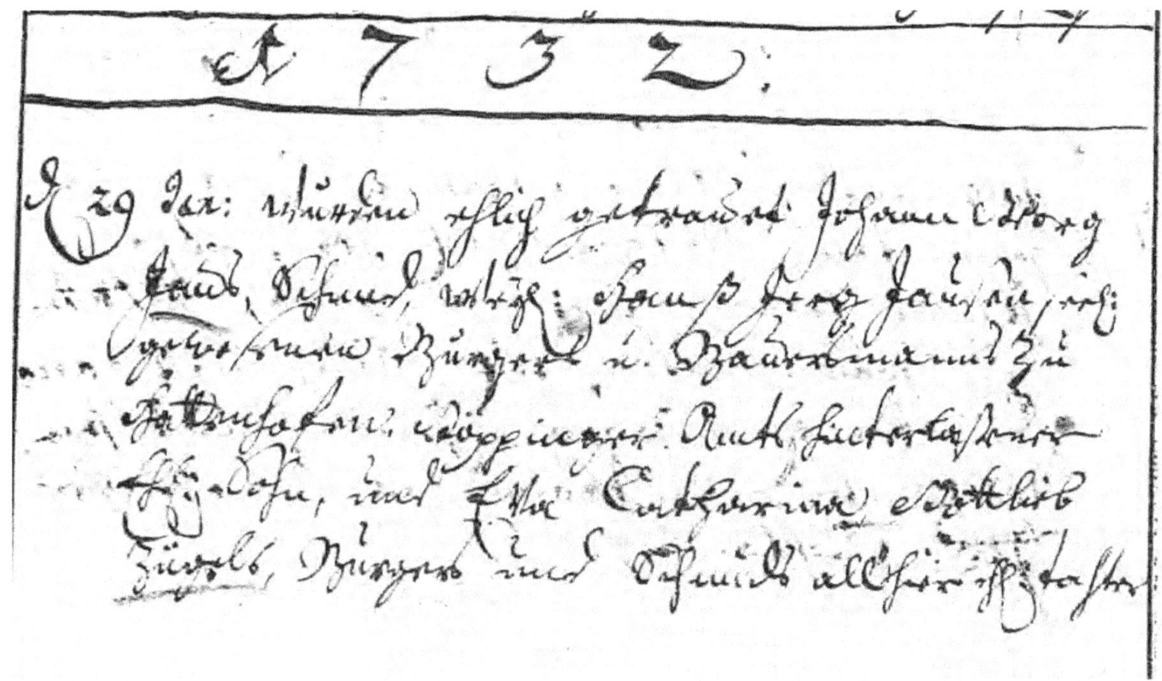



*Source: Ancestry.com*

Hans Georg Jauss & his wife Eva Catharina had baptized:
1.  Sophia Catharina, born 6 Nov 1733, baptized 6 Nov 1733
2.  Georg Friderich, born 2 Oct 1735, baptized 2 Oct 1735
3.  Jacob, born 17 Sep 1737
4.  Johannes, born – Dec 1738 (day of birth in fold—not readable on microfilm)

Married 6 June 1769: Sophia Jaus, daughter of Johann Georg Jaus, and Bernhardt Daub.

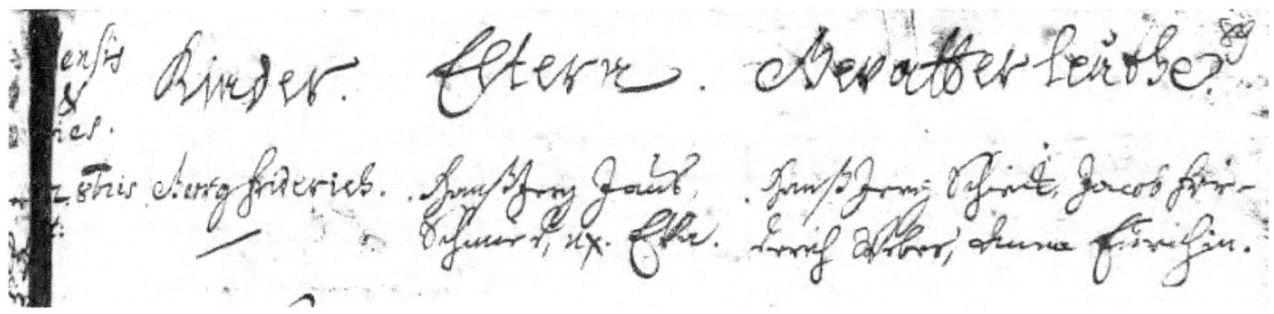

*Above: 1735 Kleingartach baptismal record for Georg Friderich Jauss (Source: Ancestry.com)*

IMMIGRATION:

**Ship *Nancy*, qualified 27 Sep 1752 at Philadelphia:**

Jacob Bauerschmid
Jacob Bauerschmidt
Gerg Friderich Jauss

PENNSYLVANIA RECORDS:

**_York (Christ) Lutheran KB, York County, Pennsylvania:_**

_Note: At the time of this compilation, I do not have access to either the original records or a complete church transcript. According to other researchers, Georg Friederich Jauss married 15 Aug 1758 to Anna Catharina Fackler._

Frederick Jauss & his wife Catharina had baptized:
1. Johann Jacob, born 3 June 1759, baptized 10 June 1759—died 15 Aug 1760
2. Anna Barbara, born 27 Nov 1760, baptized, baptized 7 Dec 1760
3. Jacob Frederick, born 25 Feb 1762, baptized 28 Feb 1762
4. Anna Catharina, born 18 Jan 1764, baptized 22 Jan 1764
5. Johann George, born 23 Feb 1767, baptized 8 Mar 1767
6. Johann Philipp, born 3 Jan 1772, ,baptized 12 Jan 1772
7. Anna Elisabeth, born 18 Apr 1774, baptized 8 May 1774
8. Johannes, born 26 May 1777, baptized 22 June 1777
9. Michael, born 11 Feb 1782, baptized 10 Mar 1782
10. Magdalena, born 6 Oct 1785, baptized 23 Oct 1785

Frederick Jauss & his wife Salome had baptized:
1. Samuel, born 20 Oct 1788, baptized 9 Nov 1788

# Casper Krüger (or Krieger)

**1730 Thistle**

Annette K. Burgert previously documented Casper Krieger's marriage and emigration in her work entitled *Eighteen Century Emigrants from the Northern Kraichgau*. In that volume, she did not include abstracts of Kleingartach records.


GERMAN RECORDS:

### Kleingartach Evangelisch KB:

Ernest Krieger & his wife Christina had baptized:
1. Ernestus, born 6 Jan 1688, baptized 6 Jan 1688
2. Agnes Maria, born Oct 1689, baptized Oct 1689

Hans Ernst Krieger (or Krueger) married 1 June 1690 Anna Catharina Werner, the daughter of Valentin Werner. They had baptized:
1. Ernestina, born 4 Feb 1691, baptized 5 Feb 1691
2. Agnes Maria, born 8 Jan 1693, baptized 8 Jan 1693
3. Eva Elisabetha, born 14 July 1695, baptized 15 July 1695
4. Eva, baptized 28 June 1697
5. Anna Catharina, baptized 28 Jan 1699
6. Johann Casper, born 25 July 1702, baptized 26 July 1702
7. Johann Heinrich, born 15 Feb 1705, baptized 15 Feb 1705
8. Barbara, born 2 Apr 1707, baptized 3 Apr 1707
9. Eva Christina, born 19 Nov 1709, baptized 20 Nov 1709
10. Hans Veltin, born 4 Apr 1712, baptized 4 Apr 1712

Ernestina Krieger, daughter of Ernst Krieger, married 6 June 1714 Johannes Holtzwart

Catharina Krieger, daughter of Johann Ernst Krieger, married 26 Feb 1726 Balthas Marbach


### Schwaigern Evangelisch KB:

Married 17 Aug 1728: Johann Casper Krieger, weaver, son of the late Ernst Krieger, citizen and baker at Klein Gartach, and Anna Christina, daughter of Hans Jerg Hoffert. They had baptized:
1. Philipp Casper, born 5 Sep 1729

IMMIGRATION:

**Ship *Thistle*, qualified 29 Aug 1730 at Philadelphia:**

Peter Trawiener
Caspar Krieger
Bernhard Renn
Dieterich Kober


PENNSYLVANIA RECORDS:

***Stoever, Rev. John Casper, personal register:***

Caspar Kreuger (Oley Mountains) had baptized:
1.  George Valentine, born 9 Feb 1734, baptized 2 Mar 1734, sp. John George Hoffert


***New Hanover Lutheran KB, Montgomery County, Pennsylvania:***

Casper Kruger & his wife Christina had baptized:
1.  Georg, born 27 Sep 1747, baptized 21 Mar 1748—died 5 Oct 1748

Confirmed 29 Mar 1752:
Valentin Krüger, Casper's son, aged 12 year [sic]

Confirmed 20 May 1753:
Adam Krüger, Casper Kruger's son, aged 15 years
Anna Catharina, Krügerin, Casper Kruger's daughter, aged 13 years

***Frederick County, Maryland, Will A254:***

Casper Kreeger of Frederick County in the Province of Maryland, writ 6 Sep 1763, probated 1 Oct 1765.
1.  He makes provisions for his wife Christina.
2.  To his son Henry: The plantation whereon I now live.
3.  The residue of my land and the rest to his other children equally, viz. Christian, Conrad, Adam, Michael, George, Valentine, and Catharina.
4.  Adds clarification that all children shall share equally in the total valuation of the lands.
5.  Executors: Wife Christina and son Valentine.
6.  Signed his name as Caspar Kruger.

***Frederick County, Maryland Vol. P, page 493, dated 6 Jul 1772, and recorded 2 Dec 1772:***

At the request of Adam Creager, son of Caspar Creager, and his will dated 5 Sep 1763 among his bequests and legacies, bequeathed unto his sons and daughter, namely: Christian, Conrad, Adam, Michael, George, Valentine, Catherine, and Henry........ This indenture between Valentine, Conrad, Michael, and George Creager and Jacob Fout, who intermarried with Catherine Creager, Adam. Wives who relinquished their dower rights were Christiana, wife of Valentine; Mary, wife of Conrad; Margaret, wife of Michael; and Catherine, wife of George.

# Johannes Küntzler

A Johannes Kienzler from Kl. Gartach (Kleingartach) died in Lancaster in 1755 as a single man. In the Kleingartach church records, I found only one Küntzler family. No person named Johannes Kuntzler, et al., who fits the immigrant profile was found; however, it may be possible that one of two sons of Matthäus Küntzler—Johann Matthäus and Johann Adam—could have been the man who died in Lancaster. In the Kleingartach baptismal register, these children have no crosses next to their names, suggesting that they lived to adulthood. I found no further record of them in the church book.

GERMAN RECORDS:

***Kleingartach Evangelisch KB:***

Mathias Küntzler & his wife Anna Maria had baptized:
1. Maria Christina, born 15 Sep 1716
2. Gottliebin, born 2 April 1717 (cross next to child's name)
3. Maria Catharina, born 21 July 1720, baptized 22 July 1720—died 24 Jan 1721
4. Johannes, born 15 Dec 1721, baptized 15 Dec 1721—died 23 Dec 1721
5. Joh. Friderich, born 5 Mar 1723, baptized 6 Mar 1723
6. Johann Matthäus, born 22 Aug 1726, baptized 23 Aug 1726
7. Philippina, born 23 Sep 1729—died 25 Oct 1750
8. Johann Adam, born 20 Feb 1734

Died 7 Mar 1751: Matthäus Kentzler, schmid, aged 61 years, 5 months

Married 30 July 1743: Maria Christina Kintzler, daughter of Matthaus Kintzler, and Conrad Steinrick

Married 26 Jan 1751: Gottliebin Kentzler, daughter of Matthaeus Kentzler, *burger und huffschmid* here, and Johann Georg Nagelin, schmid, son of Jacob Nagelin, *burger und schmid zu Stetten*

Married 5 Nov 1749: Johann Friderich Kintzler, son of Johann Matthai Kintzler, *burgerlich inwohner und hufschmid*, and Maria Barbara, daughter of Michael Schodel, burger zu Pfafenhofen

Johann Friderich Küntzler burger u. weingartner here, & his wife Elisabetha Barbara had baptized:
1. Johann Christoph, born – Dec 1749 (day of birth in fold—not readable on microfilm)
2. Johann Friderich, born 26 Mar 1752 (cross next to name)
3. Alexander, born 25 Jan 1754, baptized 25 Jan 1754
4. Elisabetha Rosina, born 5 Mar 1756, baptized 7 Mar 1756
5. Johann Adam, born 15 June 1758, baptized 16 June 1758
6. Christina Barbara, born 8 Mar 1760, baptized 9 Mar 1760

*--Note: Mother's name given only as Barbara at baptism of son Christoph. Also, the marriage abstract below is found in familysearch—however, I see no marriage of this couple on that date. It was added to a batch file of Kleingartach records. The original source is unclear.*

Married 19 Oct 1749: Johann Friderich Kentzler, son of Matthaus Kentzler, and Elisabeth Barbara Schedel, daughter of Michael Schedel


IMMIGRATION:

*For consideration only:*

This is the only Philadelphia arrival with the Küntzler surname found within the target search period. This man cannot be the Friedrick Kuntzler of Kleingartach.

**Ship *Brothers*, qualified 26 Sep 1753 at Philadelphia:**

Michael ( ) Snider, on board
Friderich Limbach
Friedrich Küntzler
Johannes Steidle
Hanns Jörg Fischer
Johannes Mann


PENNSYLVANIA RECORDS:

***Lancaster Lutheran KB, Lancaster County, Pennsylvania:***

Johannes Kienzler, from Kl[ein] Gartach, single, died 9 Aug 1755, buried the following day

# Ezekial Ocker

**1743 St. Andrew**

Ezekial Ocker appears to have been a single man at the time of his emigration. An Ezekial Ocker married the Widow Wurster at Kleingartach in 1729; however, evidence suggests they were both born circa 1680. After the elder Ezekial Ocker's death in 1734, his widow married again in 1736.

In the earliest records, the surname also appears as Okker and Ockher.

The immigrant Ezekial Ocker died leaving neither a widow nor children. His estate descended to his sister Maria Barbara and her husband Melchior Bierly (q.v.)

GERMAN RECORDS:

*Kleingartach Evangelisch KB:*

Hans Martin Ockher (or Oker) & his wife Anna Barbara Schmid had baptized:
1. Magdalena Regina, born 28 Feb 1703, baptized 2 Mar 1703
2. Ezechiel, born 11 June 1706, baptized 12 June 1706
3. Maria Catharina, born 2 Jan 1709, baptized 3 Jan 1709
4. Maria Barbara, born April 1711, baptized April 1711

Johann Melchior Bihrlen [sic] married 15 July 1738 Maria Barbara Ocker, daughter of Martin Ocker (q.v.)

IMMIGRATION:

**Ship *St. Andrew*, qualified 7 Oct 1743 at Philadelphia:**

Hans Gerg (X) Amon, age 38
Melchior Bührle, age 30
Etielle Acker, age 39 (given as Ezekial on List A)
Johannes (HU) Ulrich, age 38
Frederick (X) Hubely, age 25

PENNSYLVANIA RECORDS:

***Philadelphia County, Pennsylvania, Administration Records:***

Ezekiel Ocker, 1757, Estate No. 61.
1. Administration Bond, dated 21 Oct 1757, granted to Melchior Bierly & his wife Maria Barbara (the next of kin to Ezekial Ocker, deceased, yeoman, of Springfield Township, Bucks County). Sureties: John Weissman, nailer, of the City of Philadelphia and John Doe, gentleman, of the same place.
2. [only document in file]

# Mattheus Plantz

**1742 Francis and Elizabeth**

Lancaster County, Pennsylvania, Moravian records identify and prove this Kleingartach emigrant family. Mattheus Plantz arrived at Philadelphia aboard the Ship Francis and Elizabeth. Several weeks earlier, a Christoph Plantz and Lorentz Plantz arrived on the Ship Loyal Judith. Christoph is likely the person of this name who was taxed in East Hanover Township, Lancaster County, in 1754. His age on the ship passenger list matches the age of Mattheus Plantz's brother Christoph baptized at Kleingartach. I could find no evidence of Christoph Plantz in the Kleingartach records apart from his baptism. The pastor made no indication of death next to this entry.

It would seem strange that brothers would board different ships to travel together to the New World; however, there can always be a reasonable explanation. Further research may confirm or disprove this possibility.

In some Lancaster church translations, the surname appears as *Pflantz*. Further, researchers should note that surname can appear in German records as *Planz*, *Plantz*, *Blanz*, or *Blantz*. When searching, Soundex will return different results for these words.


GERMAN RECORDS:

***Evangelisch, Kleingartach, Neckarkreis, Baden-Württemberg:***

Hans Jacob Planz, *wagner*, & his wife Anna Margaretha, nee Boger, had baptized:
1. Anna Maria Catharina, born 10 Apr 1692, baptized 11 Apr 1692
2. Agnes Maria, born 19 May 1696
3. Anna Maria, baptized 17 Aug 1697
4. Hans Jacob, baptized 31 May 1699
5. Johann Mattheus, baptized 30 Jan 1702
6. Anna Rosina, born 22 Oct 1703, baptized 22 Oct 1703
7. Johann Christoph, born 16 Mar 1708, baptized 16 Mar 1708

*Note: I checked the church book page-by-page but found no baptism for this couple from 1693 to 1695.*

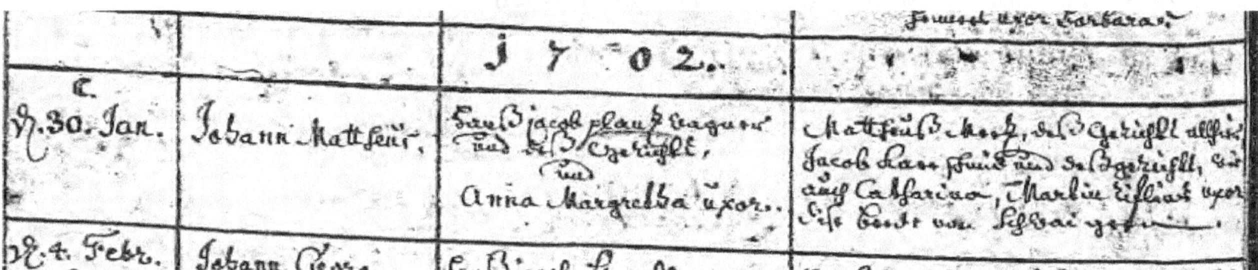

Hans Jerg Hermann & his wife Ernestina Anastasia, nee Waldeysin, had baptized:
1. Johanna Justina, born 22 Nov 1702, baptized 22 Nov 1702

Married 14 May 1726: Johann Mathaeus Plantz, *Schmid*, son of Jacob Plantz, *wagner*, married 14 May 1726 Johanna Justina, daughter of Joh. Georg Herman.

Mattheus Plantz (or Blantz) & his wife Johanna Justina had baptized:
1.  Johann Mathaeus, born 22 Oct 1728, baptized 23 Oct 1728
2.  Christoff Ulrich, baptized 8 Jan 1733 (cross next to name)
3.  Christina Barbara, baptized 8 Nov 1733
4.  Ernestina, born – Dec 1735 (cross next to name)
5.  Justina Margaretha, born 24 Oct 1736 (cross next to name)
6.  Johannes, born – Dec 1738 (cross next to name)
7.  Ernestina, born 30 Mar 1741, baptized 30 Mar 1741


IMMIGRATION:


**Ship *Loyal Judith*, qualified 3 Sep 1742 at Philadelphia:**

Samuel Fortineaux, age 17
Lorentz (LB) Place, age 44
Christohf Plantz, age 32 (Surname *Place* on List A)
Christohf Bergman, age 30
Johanes Rühl, age 38
Ludwig Metzger, age 40

**Ship *Francis and Elisabeth*, qualified 21 Sep 1742 at Philadelphia:**

Adam Seibert
Hans Jerg Knödler
Hans Michel (H) Bouer
Johann Mattheis Plantz
Johanes Grob
Philip (H) Shleyhouff


PENNSYLVANIA RECORDS:


***Lancaster County, Pennsylvania, Tax Records:***

Christopher Plantz, 1754, East Hanover Township
Mathias Plantz, 1759, Mount Joy Township, inmate
Mathias Plantz, 1772-1782, Mount Joy Township, 3A
Mathias Plantz, 1771-1773, Elizabeth Township, inmate (rent to Chr. Stahley '71)


***Warwick (Emanuel) Lutheran KB, Elizabeth Township, Lancaster County, Pennsylvania:***

Joh. Mattheis Pflantz had baptized:
1. Anna Elisabeta, born 14 Jan 1744, baptized 12 Feb 1744, sp. Johannes Stör & his wife Margaretha
2. Catharina Margaretha, born 16 Oct 1746, baptized 21 Oct 1746, sp. Joh. Christoph Süss and his fiancée Catharina Elisabetha Haagerin; Joh. Wilhelm Stober and his fiancée Anna Margaretha Süssin


***Stoever, Rev. John Casper, personal register:***

Married 1 Feb 1748 at the Warwick congregation: Mattheis Pflantz and Elisabetha Balmer
Married 19 June 1758 at the Derry congregation: Anna Catharina Pflantz and John George Dumm
Married 10 July 1764 at the Donegal congregation: Anna Elisabeth Pflantz and John Jacob Bohrmann
Married 28 May 1771 at the Lebanon congregation: Christina Pflantz and Andrew Beistel


***Lancaster (Trinity) Lutheran KB, Lancaster, Lancaster County, Pennsylvania:***

Mathaeus Blantz & his wife Elisabetha had baptized:
1. Johannes Benjamin, born 21 Oct 1748, baptized 29 Jan 1749, sp. Benjamin Spieker & his wife Margaretha Barbara


***Hill Lutheran KB, Lebanon County, Pennsylvania:***

Matthias Pflantz & his wife Elisabeth had baptized:
1. Juliana, born – Feb 1750, baptized 18 Mar 1750, sp. John Grasser & Catharina Kueffer
2. Rosina, born 21 Mar 1751, baptized 25 Mar 1751, sp. William Stober & his wife; also, Christopher Suess & his wife
3. Catharina (twin), born 11 Apr 1753, baptized 17 Apr 1753, sp. George Buerger & his wife Catharina and Michael Gassel & his wife Anna Mary.
4. Anna Maria (twin), born 11 Apr 1753, see above

Barbara Pflantz and Michael Firnsler sponsored child of Jacob & Anna Catharina Stober on 26 Dec 1751

Christina Pflantz married 28 May 1771 Andrew Beistel


***Donegal/Mount Joy Moravian KB, Lancaster County, Pennsylvania***

Catalogue of Families

39 & 40. Matthes Pflanz, shoemaker, born in 1729 at Klein Gartach, Württemberg. Lutheran. He married 29 Sep 1767 Elisabeth, nee Göpfertin, born 26 June 1749 (the daughter of 17 & 18 Georg and Elisabeth Göpfert). They were accepted into the Moravian congregation in 1774. [List of children follows.]

3 Oct 1797. Elisabeth Pflanzin; born 26 June 1749 near here. She married in 1767 Matheus Pflantz. 13 children, of whom 1 sons and 2 daughters have died, and 3 grandchildren. Her age: 48 years, 3 months, 6 days.

8 Oct 1797. Mathias Pflantz, single, born 8 Oct 1773. Age 24 years less 1 day.

15 Nov 1797. Johannes Pflantz, single, born 5 Jan 1771. Age 26 years, 10 months, 10 days.

29 Jan 1802. Mattheus Pflanz, born 22 Oct 1729 Kleingartach. He married Elis. Göpfertin; she died 4 years ago. They had 13 children, of whom 5 have died and 8 survive. He was a full communicant of the Moravians; however, his sons were quite vicistudinous, because of their drinking. His age: 72 years, 3 months.

*Family Register*

Mattheus Pflanz - Elisabeth Goepfert

Mattheus Pflanz was born at Kleingartach, Wuerttemberg, Germany 22 Oct 1729.
He married Elisabeth Goepfert 13 Oct 1767 at Mount Joy, Lancaster, Pennsylvania . Elisabeth Goepfert was born at Mount Joy, Lancaster, Pennsylvania 26 Jun 1749 daughter of Georg Goepfert and Elisabeth Brodbeck .

They were the parents of 13 children:
Elisabeth Pflanz born 4 Aug 1768.
Christina Pflanz born 23 Dec 1769.
Johannes Pflanz born 5 Jan 1771.
Christina Pflanz born 3 Mar 1772.
Mattheus Pflanz born 9 Oct 1773.
Johan Jacob Pflanz born 3 Feb 1775.
Anna Maria Pflanz born 18 Jul 1777.
Salome Pflanz born 28 Feb 1779.
Catharina Pflanz born 11 Oct 1781.
Magdalena Pflanz born 12 Mar 1784.
Barbara Pflanz born 12 Jan 1788.
Barbara Pflanz born 13 Jun 1789.
Susanna Pflanz born 18 Feb 1791.

Mattheus Pflanz died 29 Jan 1802 at Mount Joy, Lancaster, Pennsylvania .
Elisabeth Goepfert died 3 Oct 1797 at Mount Joy, Lancaster, Pennsylvania .

*Lancaster County, Pennsylvania, Wills:*

Lancaster Will C245: The will of Mathias Plantz was written in German and could not be recorded. More than a century later, the original German will was transcribed and entered into Book Y2. I do not have access to this book at the time of writing. An abstract under the direction of the Genealogical Society of Pennsylvania gives the following information:

Lancaster Will Y2-504:
PLANTZ, MATHIAS, yeoman, of Elizabeth Township, writ 5 Apr 1774, probated 20 June 1774
1. Wife: Elizabeth Blantz.
2. Children: George, Barbara, Margaret, Elizabeth, Juliana, Rosina, Ann and Catharine.
3. Executors: Jacob Neef and Elizabeth Blantz.

*--Note: These will abstracts are notoriously incomplete and frequently omit names and relationships. It may be that Mathias provided for the surviving children of his first wife and—by this testament—makes provisions for his younger children by his second wife.*

# Rudolff Reichardt

**1732 Pink Plaisance**

According to descendants, the surname evolved to Ryherd or Ryher. They identify Rudolph's son Adam as the Adam Riherd of Franklin County, Virginia, whose last will & testament was probated in 1823.


GERMAN RECORDS:

***Evangelisch, Endersbach, Neckarkreis, Baden-Württemberg:***

(FHC Film 1056991)

Hans Adam Reichardt & his wife Euphrosina had baptized:
1. Johannes, baptized 4 Sep 1677
2. Hans Adam, baptized 3 Feb 1679
3. Johannes, baptized 18 Aug 1681
4. Daniel, baptized 5 Dec 1682
5. Rudolph, baptized 25 Jan 1686
6. Johannes, baptized 29 Feb 1688
7. Maria Catharina, baptized 4 July 1691

***Evangelisch, Kleingartach, Neckarkreis, Baden-Württemberg:***

Rudolph Reichert, son of Adam Reichert, married 24 Sep 1709 Esther Taub, daughter of Jacob Taub. They had baptized:
1. Euphrosina, born 10 Aug 1710, baptized 11 Aug 1710
2. Agnes Maria, born 2 Aug 1711, baptized 2 Aug 1711
3. Maria Gottliebin, born 11 Jan 1713, baptized 11 Jan 1713
4. Esther, born 21 Oct 1715, baptized 22 Oct 1715
5. Maria Juditha, born 14 May 1717, baptized 15 May 1717
6. Anna Catharina, born 26 Oct 1718, baptized 28 Oct 1718
7. Johann Georg, born 28 Aug 1721, baptized 29 Aug 1721
8. Johann Jacob, born 23 Sep 1724, baptized 24 Sep 1724
9. Christina, born 28 July 1727, baptized 29 July 1727
10. Sabina, born 17 Sep 1728, baptized 17 Sep 1728


IMMIGRATION:

**Pink *Plaisance*, qualified 21 Sep 1732 at Philadelphia:**

Rudolff Reichert, age 46 (signed his name)
Hester Rigard, age 43
Maria Gotliven Ricarten, age 17
Ronyard Richards (age not given on children's list)

PENNSYLVANIA RECORDS:

***Philadelphia County, Pennsylvania, Estate Records:***

Philadelphia Will O456:
Rudolph Reichard of Lower Milford Township, Bucks County, written 24 Jan 1770, probated 8 Feb 1770.
1.  He makes provisions for his wife Esther. She may continue to reside in their dwelling house for the rest of her natural life.
2.  To my eldest son George Reichard: The sum of ten pounds prior to the equal division of my estate.
3.  To my second son Adam: The sum of ten pounds aforesaid.
4.  To my daughter Sabina: The sum of eleven pounds aforesaid. "She shall stay with her child by her mother as my said wife Esher as long as my wife liveth…."
5.  The half part of the hereditary share of my daughter Gottliebin shall be given to her daughter Albertina and the other half share remain her hereditary share."
6.  After the death of my wife my plantation and whatever remains of my estate shall be divided into equal parts.
7.  "…as I rented out my plantation to Jacob Long to be tilled by him so shall his bargain shall be held out."
8.  Executors: Daniel Miller and my Son Adam Reicherd
9.  Witnessed by Henry Huber and George Lohness.

# Adam Sorg

**1752 President**

In 1755, the widower Adam Sorg from "Klein Gartach" remarried at Lancaster (Trinity) Lutheran Church in Lancaster County, Pennsylvania. In the Kleingartach church records, I find only one Adam Sorg, born in 1705. This Adam Sorg had three children baptized there from 1734 to 1737; thereafter, I found no further evidence of his residence.

GERMAN RECORDS:

***Evangelisch, Kleingartach, Neckarkreis, Baden-Württemberg:***

Mattheus Sorg & his wife Anna Barbara, nee Danckler, had baptized:
1.  Hans Michael, born 17 Feb 1704, baptized 18 Feb 1704
2.  Hans Adam, born 17 Jan 1705, baptized 17 Jan 1705
3.  Johann Leonhard, born 5 Oct 1707, baptized 6 Oct 1707
4.  Matthaues, born 14 Feb 1710, baptized 14 Feb 1710
5.  Joseph Martin, born 1712
6.  Gottlieb, born Feb 1716
7.  Hans Jerg, born 23 June 1718, baptized 24 June 1718

Died 21 Oct 1766: Mattheüs Sorg, aged 87 years

Adam Sorg & his wife Eva Rosina, Reformed, had baptized:
1.  Michael, born August 1734, sp. Michael Weissert, Michel Nagel & Juliana, Leonhart Sorgen of Guglingen
2.  Mattheus, born -- June 1736 (cross next to name), sp. Michael Weissert, Michel Nagel, Leonhart Sorgen of Guglingen, Julianna
3.  Eva Barbara, born 2 Sep 1737, sp. Leonhart Sorg of Guglingen and Catharina Nagelin

***Guglingen Evangelisch KB:***

Married 13 July 1734: Johann Leonhard Sorg, son of Johann Michael Sorgen [sic], citizen at Kleinen Gartach, and Juliana Barbara, daughter of Johannes Schmaussen

IMMIGRATION:

**Ship *President*, qualified 27 Sep 1752 at Philadelphia:**

Johann Georg Wagner
Johann Heinrich Kostenbader
Adam Sorg
Johanes (X) Faber
Peter (+) Paltzly


PENNSYLVANIA RECORDS:

***Lancaster Lutheran KB:***

Married 8 Apr 1755: Adam Sorg, joiner, widower, from Klein Gartach, and Catharina Brehmerin


***Lancaster Reformed KB:***

Adam Sorg & his wife sponsored child of James Strong & his wife Magdalena on 9 Aug 1768.


*For consideration:*

***Strayer's Reformed KB, Dover Township, York County, Pennsylvania:***

Mattheis Sorg & his wife Christina had baptized:
1. Dorothea Eva, born 2 Apr 1768, baptized 22 May 1768, sp. Leonhard Stauch & Dorothea Hartman
2. Johan Adam, born 28 Sep 1770, baptized 14 Oct 1770, sp. Frederick & Charlotta Stauch
3. Eva Elisabeth, born 5 Mar 1773, baptized 7 Mar 1773, sp. Christopher & Maria Dorothea Cober


*Of interest:*

***New Hanover Lutheran KB:***

Adam Sorg & his wife Anna Maria had baptized:
1. Eva, born 3 Apr 1761, baptized 26 Apr 1761, sp. Valentine Stichter & his wife
2. Joh. Adam, born 1 Jan 1763, baptized 18 Jan 1763, sp. Philip Sorg
3. Anna Maria, born 19 Nov 1764, baptized 9 Dec 1764, sp. Ludwig Weigel & his wife Anna Maria
4. Anna Elisabeth, born 8 Dec 1766, baptized 1 Mar 1767, sp. Valentin Schichter & his wife Anna Eva


*The Sorg family members of Montgomery County appear distinct from the Lancaster-York line. The 1752 immigrant Dietrich Sorg may be the father. See the 1771 Philadelphia County estate file for Adam Sorg of Douglass Township.*

# George Frederick Zugel

# Gottlieb Zugel

**1743 St. Andrew**

Gottlieb Zügel of Kleingartach had four children or grandchildren who went to America:
1. Daughter Eva Catharina's son Georg Friederich Jauss (q.v.)
2. Son Georg Friederich Zügel and his family.
3. Son Gottlieb Zügel.
4. Daughter Maria Catharina and her husband Jacob Bauerschmid (q.v.)

With the exception of Jacob Bauerschmid, whose place of rest could not be determined, the others lived and died in York County, Pennsylvania. Descendants are in possession of a family bible, and the family in America has been well researched (see selections below).


GERMAN RECORDS:

***Evangelisch, Kleingartach, Neckarkreis, Württemberg:***

Gottlieb Zugel, son of Heinrich Zugel, married 15 July 1704 Anna Catharina Seelichland. They had baptized:
1. Catharina Barbara, born 26 Aug 1705, baptized – Aug 1705—died 30 May 1706
2. Eva Catharina, born 21 July 1707, baptized 22 July 1707
3. Jerg Heinrich, born 5 Sep 1709, baptized 6 Sep 1709
4. Hans Jacob, born 12 Dec 1710, baptized 12 Dec 1710
5. Maria Margaretha, born 6 Feb 1712, baptized 6 Feb 1712
6. Juliana, born 22 Sep 1715, baptized 22 Sep 1715—died 23 Feb 1716 (Her mother is identified as Anna Catharina Weisert.)
7. Jerg Fridrich, born 1 Apr 1717, baptized 2 Apr 1717
8. Johann Gottlieb, born 29 Feb 1720, baptized 1 Mar 1720
9. Johann Conradt, born 6 Aug 1722, baptized 7 Aug 1722—died 26 Jan 1790
10. Elisabeth Barbara, born 14 Apr 1728, baptized 14 Apr 1728

*--Note: Marriage records indicate a daughter Maria Catharina likely born 1724-1727; however, I did not locate a baptismal entry for her.*

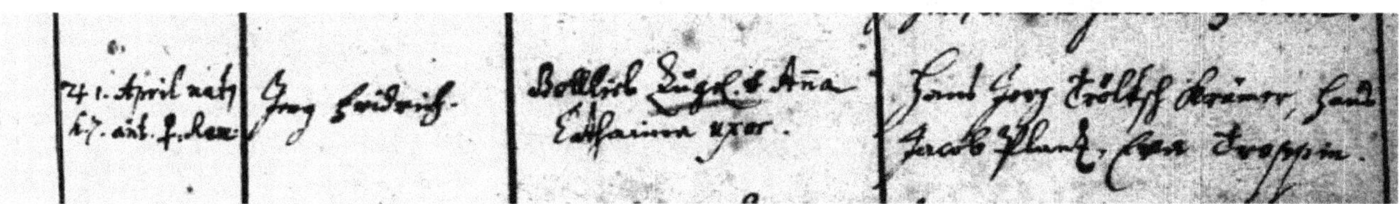

*Above: 1717 baptismal record for American immigrant Georg Friedrich Zugel. Below, 1720 baptismal record for American immigrant Gottlieb Zugel. (Source: Ancestry.com)*

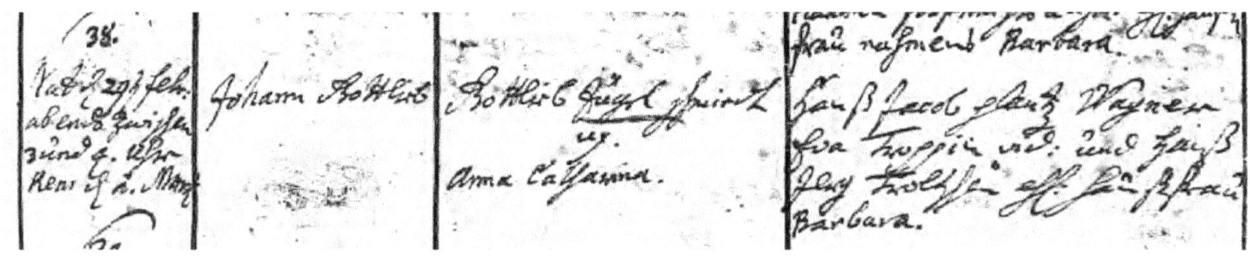

Married 29 Jan 1732: Eva Catharina Zugel, daughter of Gottlieb Zugel, and Johann Georg Jaus, son of Hans Jerg Jaus

Married 7 Feb 1736: Maria Margaretha Zugel, daughter of Gottlieb Zugel, and Hans Michael Eurich, son of Hans Michael Eurich

Married 28 Apr 1739: Georg Friderich Zugel, son of Gottlieb Zugel, and Anna Margaretha Schieber, daughter of Hans Jerg Schieber.

Married 30 Apr 1748: Johann Conrad Zugel, son of Gottlieb Zugel, and Eva Mauderer, daughter of Jacob Mauderer

Married 23 July 1748: Maria Catharina Zugel, daughter of Gottlieb Zugel, and Jacob Bauerschmeid


Georg Friderich Zugel & his wife Anna Margaretha had baptized:
1. Johann Michael, born 3 July 1739
2. Johann Georg, born 22 Feb 1742, baptized 22 Feb 1742


IMMIGRATION:

**Ship *St. Andrew*, qualified 7 Oct 1743 at Philadelphia:**

List C:

Leonhart (X) Dewalt, age 28
Jacob Wayst, age 28 [appears on List A at this placement but not List C]
Hans Adam (X) Sommer, age 27
Gorg Fridrich Zügel
Gottlieb (X) Zigel,

Johan (X) Mergel, age 25
Gottlieb Schlees[eis], age 26 [Godliph Leweys on List A]
Jacob (X) Clausser, age 25

*--Above: I merged Lists C (which has passenger signatures) with List A, which includes passenger ages. The Zügel brothers do not appear on List A at the same placement in which they signed List C.*

List A:

Fredk. Doughtermann, age 22
Andreas Doughtermann, age 18
Ernest Ament, age 35
Fredk Ziegell, age 26
Hans Jacob Golder, age 33
Hans Geo. Ament, age 38
Melchior Beerlie, age 30
Ezekiel Ocher, age 39
Johannes Ulrich, age 38
John Fredk. Houbley, age 35
….
Abram Hober, age 27
Phillip Brafshnyder, age 25
Valantine Shutter, age 45
Hendk Shutter, age 22
Godliph Zeigell, age 22
Phyt Reysner [no age given]
Johan Mar. Say [no age given]


PENNSYLVANIA RECORDS:

***Lancaster (Trinity) Lutheran KB, Lancaster, Lancaster County, Pennsylvania:***

Georg Friedrich Ziegel, widower, married 21 Feb 1749 Anna Margaretha, widowed Trarbachin in the church here

Peter Lorentz and Anna Margaretha Ziegelin, sister of the father, sponsored child of Johann Adam Streher & his wife Maria Catharina on 27 Mar 1749

George Friederich Ziegel & his wife Anna Margaretha sponsored child of Georg Balthasar Wecker on 8 Oct 1752

Friederich Zügel, Maria, sister, sponsored child of Johann Martin Schrenk & his wife Maria on 4 Aug 1754

Friederich Zügel & his wife Anna Margaretha sponsored child of Peter Klein & his wife Elisabeth on 10 Apr 1757

Anna Margaret, wife of Friedrich Zügel, aged 28 years, two months, died in the backwoods, 29 July 1757, was buried there honorably on July 31st.

--------------------------------------------------

Georg Friedrich Zügel, widower, blacksmith, from Klein Gartach, married 1 Nov 1757 Maria Magdalena Koehlerin, single

Friedrich Zügel & his wife Maria Magdalena had baptized:
1.  Anna Maria, born 2 Feb 1764, baptized 7 May 1764, sp. Anan Maria Laumännin
2.  Maria Susanna, born 14 Mar 1766, baptized 10 May 1766, sp. Daniel Koehler & his wife Anna Maria
3.  Jacob Friedrich, born 1 Feb 1771, baptized 9 May 1771, sp. John Nicholas Schwerdt & his wife Catharina Elisabeth


### *York County, Pennsylvania, Estate Records:*

York Will:
Gottlieb Ziegel of York Town, writ 12 Jan 1779, probated 1 Mar 1779.
1.  Wife Maria Barbara.
2.  Children Mary, Magdalena (wife of George Fry), Gottlieb, and Thomas.
3.  Executors: Frederick Zeigel and Frederick Zonce.

York Will:
George Frederick Ziegel of York Township, writ 1 May 1779, probated 21 June 1779.
1.  "being sick and weak"
2.  He makes provisions for his wife Maria Magdalena, who may continue to reside in their dwelling house on their plantation during her widowhood. Further, she shall provide for and raise the younger children. (Reference is made to a marriage contract between them.)
3.  My executors shall sell my dwelling plantation situate in York Township, adjoining the lands of Godfrey Frey, George Spangler, John Herbach, Esq., John Stuart, and others—containing about 200 acres more or less. This sale to be conducted at or before the arrival of my son Jacob Frederick Ziegel to the age of 21 years.
4.  The value of my estate to be equally divided amongst my children, to wit: Barbara, Anna Maria, Maria Susanna, Anna Christina Ziegel,  Jacob Frederick Ziegel, and Elisabeth Ziegel.
5.  Provisions are made in the event that his wife is pregnant with child.
6.  If my estate becomes indebted, then I authorize the sale of 20 acres of land (which I bought of Nicholas Scheffer at public vendue) to be divided off my plantation and sold to the best advantage.
7.  Executors: My loving and trusty friends John Herbach and Frederick Youch and my wife Maria Magdalena.
8.  Signed his name as Geo. F. Ziegel.


### *From Zugel Family Genealogists:*

Descendants of George Frederick Zugel—most notably James Spraker--have done extensive genealogical research. A transcription of the Zugel Family Bible has been posted on the Smith Genealogy website (http://www.the-sims-family.net/genealogy/index.htm). The York County Historical Society (Pennsylvania) appears to have copies of the original research.

# Possible Emigrant: Adam Seibert (or Seebert)

This family disappears from church records. On the 1742 Ship *Francis and Elisabeth*, an Adam Seibert arrived, signing near to Johann Mattheis Plantz, a known Kleingartach emigrant.

GERMAN RECORDS:

***Kleingartach Evangelisch KB:***

Johann Adam Seeber (or Seebert), son of Christoph Seeber, married 30 Jan 1720 Margaretha Elisabeth Veyl, daughter of Johann Jacob Veyl. They had baptized:
1. Anna Christina, born 20 May 1721, baptized 21 May 1721
2. Anna Christiana, born 26 June 1722, baptized 27 June 1722
3. Maria Barbara, born 30 Oct 1724, baptized 31 Oct 1724
4. Anna Catharina, born 11 Apr 1727, baptized 11 Apr 1727
5. Anna Salome, born 11 May 1729, baptized 11 May 1729
6. Hans Jacob, born 14 May 1731, baptized 15 May 1731
7. Margaretha Elisabetha, born 12 Sep 1733
8. Anna Salome, born 22 Jan 1736
9. Eva Regina, born --- Feb 1738
10. Johann Adam, born – Feb 1738
11. Juliana, born --- Jan 1742


IMMIGRATION:

*For consideration only:*

**Ship *Francis and Elisabeth*, qualified 21 Sep 1742 at Philadelphia:**

Adam Seibert
Hans Jerg Knödler
Hans Michel (H) Bouer
Johann Mattheis Plantz
Johanes Grob
Philip (H) Shleyhouff


COLONIAL RECORDS:

*For consideration only:*

***Lancaster (Trinity) Lutheran KB, Lancaster, Lancaster County, Pennsylvania:***

Communicants 27 Jul 1748:
Anna Barbara Seberin
Anna Catharina Seberin

Confirmed 4 Dec 1748: Johann Jacob Sebert

*Internet Claims*

Some online genealogies claim that Jacob Seabert of Frederick County in Virginia, whose last will and testament was probated 30 Nov 1801, is the son of Adam Seabert/Seebert of Kleingartach—however, I could not locate the supporting evidence used to draw that conclusion.

# GERMANNA

The Mid-Atlantic Colonies were not the only destination of German migrants. According to researchers of the Germanna Colony in Virginia, at least one person with connections to Kleingartach arrived there in the Second Colony of 1717(text and information below copied from the source indicated):

**Oberowisheim, Klein-Gartach**

- Sheible/Sheibley, Johann Georg, and wife Maria Eleanora Ockert; daughters Anna Martha, Anna Elisabetha

**List of Original Germanna Settlers (Virginia)**

September 10, 2013 By Germanna

Due to the prominence of Lt. Governor Alexander Spotswood in American history, much was known of his involvement with the establishment of the Germanna Settlement, but little of the German Settlers who were brought to this area with the First Colony of 1714, the Second Colony of 1717, and later groups.

The Germanna Foundation has conducted continuing research regarding these families and their descendants.

Through these efforts, significant historic data has been obtained regarding these families who bravely traveled to a new country leaving many of their friends and family behind.

Research into these families is ongoing, therefore this list represents the best information we have at the present. Further documentary research could lead to additions or deletions from this list.

The Germanna Foundation wishes to especially thank, John V. Blankenbaker, Dr. Katharine L. Brown, Cathi Clore Frost, and Barbara Price for their diligent efforts in amplifying and correcting this list.

http://germanna.org/2013/09/10/list-of-original-germanna-settlers/

oo Oberöwisheim 13.11.1692 ev.: Johann Georg Schaible, Weber <aus 3332> *11.2.1670 + . . . und Maria Eleanora Ockert <aus 1583> *Kleingartach 29.6.1670 + . . .

5 Kinder:
Anna Martha * 14.3.1697
Anna Elisabeth * 17.9.1700
Anna Maria * 18.3.1708 + 4.4.1708
Anna Maria * 15.6.1709 + 12.7.1710
Anna Maria * 24.7.1711

# Index